About the Author

Mrs. Jyoti Giramkar has 10 years of experience in VBScript. She has worked on many VBscript Projects. She has also teaching experience of 5 years in VBScript.

Her hobbies are travelling to new tourist places, watching football, cricket and learning latest technological stuff.

A special note of Thanks to My Husband

I would like to dedicate this book to my lovely husband for loving me so much and helping me write this book. Without his support, this book would not have been a reality.

Preface

This book covers all topics on VBScript. VBScript is widely used across the world.

Major topics covered in this book are.

1. Introduction to VBScript
2. Variables, data types, Arrays
3. Control statements
4. String Handling
5. Maths functions
6. Date and time functions
7. Dictionary objects
8. File handling
9. Error handling
10. Procedures and functions
11. Classes
12. Regular expressions
13. WSH
14. WMI

1. VBScript Basics

In this chapter, You will get to know about VBScript applications and also learn about how to write and execute the simple VBScript program in Windows Operating System.

1.1 VBScript Intoduction

Vbscript is a scripting language used for performing administrative tasks in system programming.
Vb script is a loosely typed language meaning we don't need to define the data type of the variables in vbscript.
It is used only on Microsoft operating system.

1.2 VBScript Applications

VbScript is used in many places.

1. In windows administrative tasks.
2. In QTP as automation testing scripting language.
3. In html pages as a client side scripting language.
4. It is also used in embedded applications
5. VBScript is also used as server side scripting language in native ASP pages with IIS Web Server.

1.3 How to execute VBScript

You can write and execute the vbscript programs on only Windows based machines. You can create the file with extension .vbs and then double click it to execute the code inside it. Below figures show how to do it on windows 7 machine.

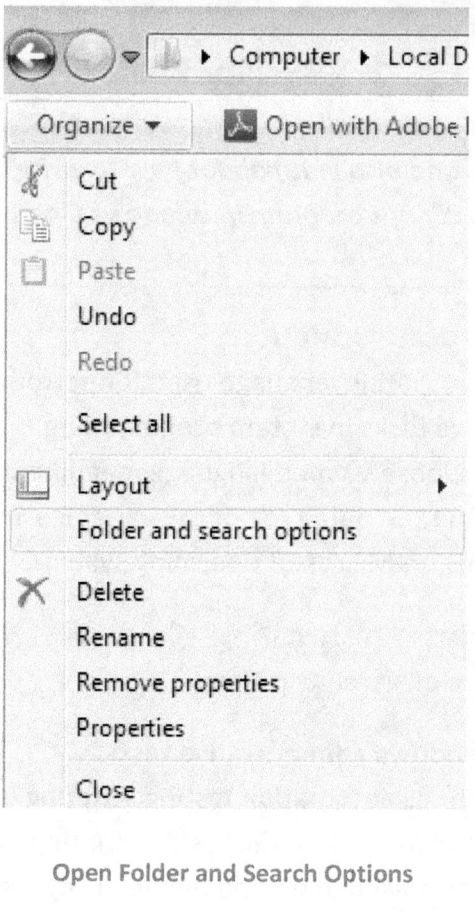

Open Folder and Search Options

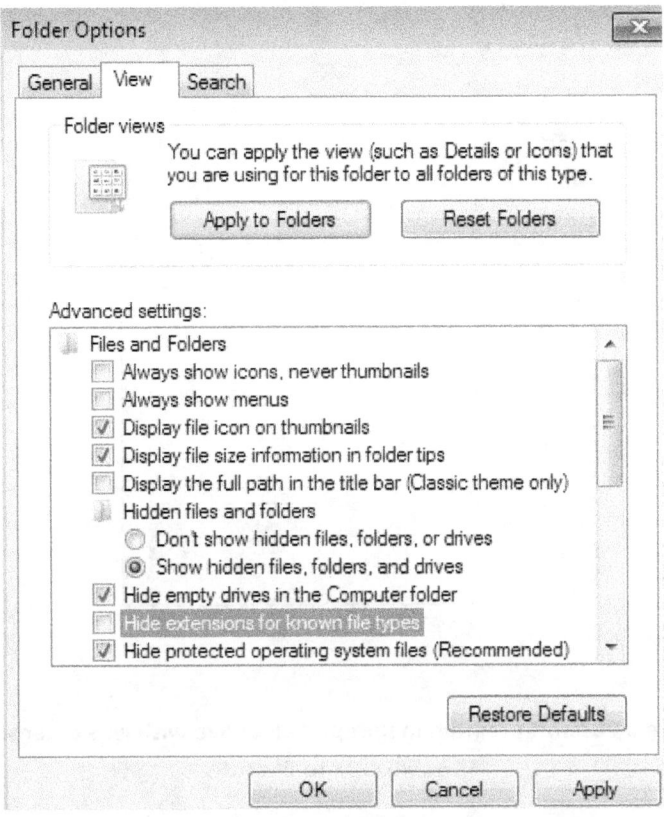

Uncheck hide extensions for known file types

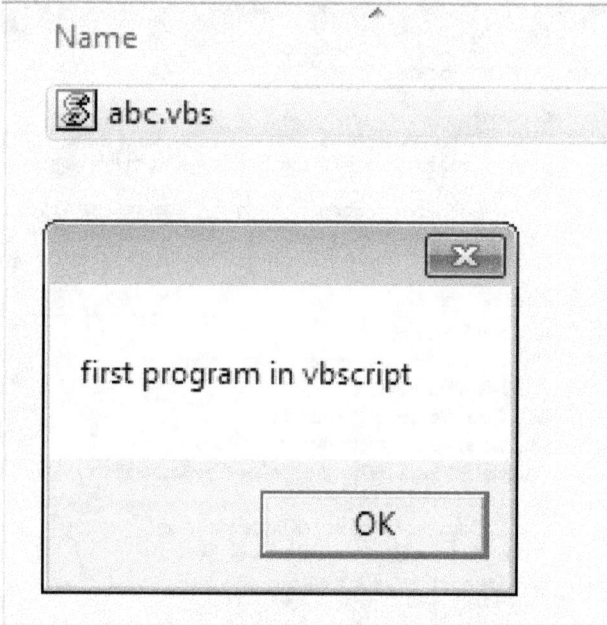

Create a vbscript program in notepad and Save with .vbs extension..
Double click to Execute

2. Variables, Data Types and Operators

In this chapter you will learn about variables, data types and operators in VBScript. You will also learn how to change the data type of the variables and find the data type of the variable.

2.1 Variables in Vbscript

Variables are storage locations in memory where we can store the values.

In vb script there are 3 types of variables.

- Scalar - contains only one value.
- Array - contains many values.
- Const - Constant variables.

Scalar variable Example in vb script -

```
Dim a
a = 10
```

In above vb script example we have a variable called a with value as 10. We can store only one value in that variable at any point of time.

Array variable Example in vb script -

```
Dim a (10)
a(1) = 22
a(4) = 23
```

In above vb script example we have a variable called a with size of 10. We can store 11 values in that variable at any point of time.

Const variable Example in vb script -
Const variable is a variable whose value does not change during the execution of the program.

```
const a=10
```

2.2 Data Types in vbscript

In vb script all variables are initialized with the data type called **variant**.

But we can have below sub data types in vb script.

In below table we have mentioned all sub data types in vb script. In next post we will see how to use these sub data types in vb script examples.

Subtype	Description
Empty	**Variable** is uninitialized. Value is 0 or ""
Null	**Variable has** Invalid data.
Boolean	True/False
Byte	Contains integer (0 to 255).

Integer	Contains integer (-32,768 to 32,767).
Currency	-922,337,203,685,477.5808 to 922,337,203,685,477.5807.
Long	Contains integer (-2,147,483,648 to 2,147,483,647).
Single	Contains a single-precision, floating-point number
Double	Contains a double-precision, floating-point number
Date (Time)	Contains a date
String	Contains a String
Object	Contains an object.
Error	Contains an error number.

Examples -

In below example we have a variable x and we have assigned a value 10 to x. In the next statement

when we use typename method to check the data type of variable x then it will show it as a integer.

```
x = 10
```

MsgBox TypeName(x) 'prints integer

```
x = 11.1
```

MsgBox TypeName(x) 'prints double

If we store the value 11.1 in the same variable x, then it's data type will be shown as Double. So this is how data type of the variables keep changing in the VBScript. So VBScript language is called as loosely typed language. And the mechanism to determine the data type of variables at runtime is called as late binding.

Data Type Conversion

We can also convert the data type of the variable explicitly using various data type conversion functions.

For example - In below code we have a VBScript which will convert the decimal number into integer.

```
a = 11.3
```

Msgbox TypeName(a) 'prints double

```
a = cint(a)
```

Msgbox Typename(a) 'prints Integer

Other data type conversion functions are.

1. cdbl - converts to double
2. cstr - converts to string
3. cbool - converts to boolean
4. cbyte - converts to byte
5. ccur - converts to currency
6. cdate - converts to date
7. clng - converts to long integer

2.3 Operators in VBScript

What are the different operators in vbscript?

At broad level there are 3 kinds of operators as mentioned below.

1. Arithmetic Operators
2. Comparison Operators
3. Logical Operators

Arithmetic Operators in the order of precedence and their usage.

- Exponentiation ^
- Unary negation –
- Multiplication *
- Floating point Division /
- Integer division \
- Modulus arithmetic Mod -gets the remainder
- Addition +
- Subtraction –
- String concatenation & - concatenates 2 strings

Comparison Operators and their usage.

- Equality =

- Inequality <>
- Less than <
- Greater than >
- Less than or equal to <=
- Greater than or equal to >=
- Object equivalence Is

Logical Operators in the order of precedence and their usage.

- Logical negation Not
- Logical conjunction And
- Logical disjunction Or
- Logical exclusion Xor
- Logical equivalence Eqv
- Logical implication Imp

Example -

```
if a>10 and b<99 then
    msgbox "a is greater than 10 and b
is less than 99"
end if

msgbox "Remainder after dividing 10 by 3
is -> " & (10 mod 3)
```

2.4 Basic Syntax in VBScript

Remember below points about VBScript Syntax.

1. VBScript is loosely typed language that means you do not need to declare the variables with data type

2. VBScript comments start with symbol '. You can also comment using rem keyword.
3. You do not need to put semicolon at the end of the statement like C,C++ and JAVA

VBScript also provides below functions that can be used to find out more information about the variables.

1. **IsArray** - This function can be used to check if the given variable is an array or not
2. **IsDate** - This function can be used to check if the given variable is a valid date or not
3. **IsEmpty** - This function can be used to check if the given variable is empty or not
4. **IsNull** - This function can be used to check if the given variable is a null or not
5. **IsNumeric** - This function can be used to check if the given variable is valid number or not
6. **IsObject** - This function can be used to check if the given variable is valid object or not
7. **TypeName** - This function returns the data type of the given variable.

Examples -

```
dim a(4)
dim b
b=10

Msgbox  "a is array? -> " & IsArray(a)
'prints true
```

```
Msgbox   "b is a date? -> " & IsDate(a)
'prints false

Msgbox   "b is empty? -> " & IsEmpty(b)
'prints false

Msgbox   "b is null? -> " & IsNull(b)
'prints false

Msgbox   "b is numeric? -> " &
IsNumeric(b)    'prints true

Msgbox   "b is object? -> " & IsObject(b)
'prints false

Msgbox   "TypeName of b -> " &
TypeName(b)    'prints integer
```

3. Control Statements

In this chapter, you will learn about various control statements in VBScript like if..else, Select...Case, For loop, For each loop, Do ..while loop.

3.1 Conditional Statements

What are different conditional statements in vbscript?

In Vbscript there are 2 types of conditional statements.

1. if ...else
2. Select Case

Example of if else -

```
a = 10

If a > 10 Then
  Msgbox "a is greater than 10"
ElseIf a>0 then
  Msgbox "a is between 0 and 11"
Else
  Msgbox "a is not greater than 0"
End If
```

Select Case Flow Chart

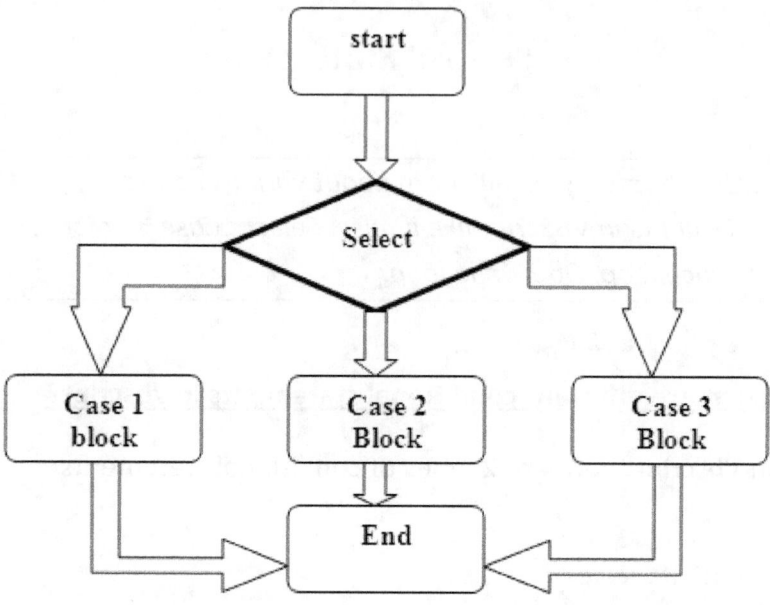

Figure 1 - Select Case Flow Chart

Example of select case -

```
a = Inputbox("enter the number")

Select Case cint(a)

    Case 1

        msgbox "You entered 1"

    Case 2
        msgbox "You entered 2"

    Case 3
        msgbox "You entered 3"
```

```
Case else
    msgbox "You entered invalid input"

End Select
```

3.2 Looping Statements

Here is the list of different looping statements in vbscript.

1. For ....Next
2. For Each ...Next
3. Do While...Loop
4. Do Until....Loop
5. While...Wend

You can exit from For Loop with Exit For statement

1) For Loop

As shown in below flowchart, we can repeat the code using for loop till the condition is true.

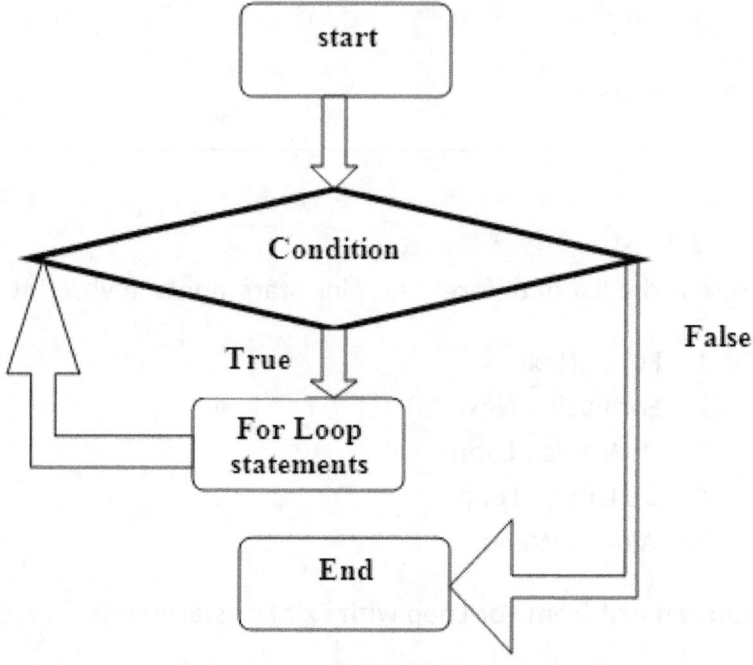

Figure 2 - For loop

```
For i=1 to 3
    Msgbox i*i
Next

'For Each loop
a   = array(22,33,5,3)
For each e in a
    Msgbox a
Next
```

You can exit from Do Loop with Exit Do statement

2) do while ...loop

```
i=1
Do while (i<3)
 Msgbox i*i
 i=i+1
Loop
```

3) do until ....loop

```
i=1
Do until i>3
 Msgbox i*i
 i=i+1
Loop
```

You can not exit from while loop using exit statement.

4) while........wend

```
i=1
While i<=3
 Msgbox i*i
 i=i+1
Wend
```

4. Arrays in VBScript

In this chapter, you will learn about Arrays in VBScript. You will learn how to declare static and dynamic arrays in VBScript. You will also learn how to access elements in the array and different operations on the array like filter, sort, join etc.

4.1 Declaring arrays in vb script

Arrays are used to store multiple values in the same variable.

We can define array in vb script in 4 different ways.

- dim a(10) - static array of 11 elements
- dim b()   - dynamic array
- a = array(1,2,3,4) - declare array with values
- a = split("as*dfdf*sdsd","*") - array is automatically created with a(0) = as, a(1)=dfdf , a(2)=sdsd

Various Operations that can be performed on the array are mentioned below

1. Iterate through all elements in the array
2. Find the lower bound and upper bound of the array
3. Filter the array
4. Join the elements in the array
5. Sort the elements in the array

1. Iterate through all elements in the array

Below example will illustrate how we can access all
elements in the array.

```
a = array(34,5,66,"sagar", 44.4)

for i=0 to ubound(a)

    'Print each element in the array one
by one.
    msgbox a(i)

next
```

2.Find the upper bound and lower bound in the array

Below example will illustrate how we can find the upper
bound and lower bound of the array.

```
a = array(34,5,66,"sagar", 44.4)
Msgbox ubound(a) 'print 4
Msgbox lbound(a) 'prints 0
```

3.Filter the array

We can use filter function to filter elements in the array.

Syntax of the Filter method is given below.
'Filter(arrayToSearch,substringToSearch[,include
[,compare]])

1. arrayToSearch - This is the array whose elements will be searched
2. substringToSearch - String to search in array
3. include - this can be true/false. If true, it will return all matching values If false, it will return all non-matching values. Default is true.
4. compare - this flag can be 0 or 1. If 0 means it will be binary comparison. else it will be textual comparison. Default is binary comparison -0

Below example will illustrate how we can filter the elements in array.

```
a = array("amol","sachin","arjun","Sagar")
b = filter(a,"s",true,0)
' b = filter(a,"s")       .....both are
same ...binary comparison....case
sensitive

for i=0 to ubound(b)

     msgbox b(i)   'will print sachin

next

'***********************************************************

a =
array("amol","sachin","arjun","Sagar")
b = filter(a,"s",true,1)

for i=0 to ubound(b)
```

```
   msgbox b(i)      'will print sachin and
Sagar........textual comparison....case
insensitive

next

'***********************************************************

a =
array("amol","sachin","arjun","Sagar")
b = filter(a,"s",false,1)

for i=0 to ubound(b)

   msgbox b(i)      'will print amol and
arjun ........non-matching elements.

Next
```

4. Join the elements in the array

Join function is used to join the elements in the array.

```
a = array("sachin", "plays", "cricket")
msgbox join(a)    'will print sachin plays
cricket
a = array("sachin", "plays", "cricket")
msgbox join(a,"*")   'will print
sachin*plays*cricket
```

4.2 Types of Array in vb script

There are 2 types of arrays in vb script.

- Static(Fixed Size)
- Dynamic

1) Static Arrays

Static array can contain fixed number of elements in array.
Example -
dim a (10) - This static array will contain only 11 elements.
If you want to increase/decrease the size of array, it will
not be possible.

2) Dynamic Arrays

In dynamic array we can change the size of array.

Dim b() - This is how we define dynamic array.
To use dynamic array we must define the size.
Redim b(5) - Array b redefined with size of 5 means it can
contain 6 elements.

22	32	1	66	8	12
0	1	2	3	4	5

Array containing 6 elements

Now if you want to increase the size of elements in array
you can use below statment

redim b(7) - In this case array can contain 8 elements but
previous elements will be erased.

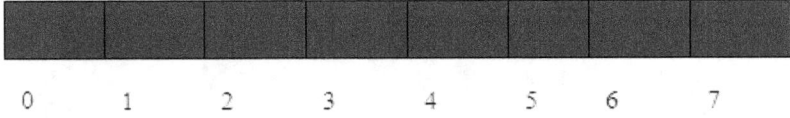

0	1	2	3	4	5	6	7

To preserve the contents of the array, we can use
Redim preserve b(7)

22	32	1	66	8	12		
0	1	2	3	4	5	6	7

When we reduce the size of dynamic array , data of the array is lost.

For example if we have a array b

```
redim preserve b(8)
```

and we execute below statement

```
redim preserve b(3)
```

Then we will not be able to access the elements at the index 4 onwards.

Erasing elements in the Array
We can use erase statement to remove the data from fixed size array. Please note that memory is still occupied by the array after erasing in fixed size array.

```
'Erasing Fixed size array
Dim a(2)
a(0)=11
Erase a
```

We can use erase statement to release the memory occupied by the **dynamic array**.

```
'Erasing Dynamic Array
Dim da()
ReDim da(2)
da(0) = 12
Erase da
```

Please note that we can have multi-dimensional arrays as well.Dim twodim(5, 10)

In above array, there will be 6 rows and 11 clolumns

5. Strings in VBScript

In this chapter, you will learn how to handle strings in VBScript. You will get to know how to find the length of string, how to convert the string to uppercase and lowercase, how to find the substring, how to remove spaces from the string, how to replace the string.

<u>String functions in vbscript</u>

Below is the list of string functions in vb script

1. lcase
2. ucase
3. len
4. left
5. right
6. mid
7. ltrim
8. rtrim
9. trim
10. replace
11. strreverse
12. string
13. Instr
14. Instrrev
15. strcomp

We are going to have a look at each String function mentioned above.

5.1 Substring Extraction functions

Some of the commonly used string manipulation functions are given below.

- right
- mid
- left

All of the above functions are frequently used when performing any string operations in vbscript.

All of the above functions extract the part of the string / Sub string.

Right function returns the fixed number of characters from right side of the string.

Left function returns the fixed number of characters from left side of the string.

Mid function can be used to get the characters/ sub string from the left, right or middle part of the string.

Examples -

```
myString = "Sachin Plays Cricket"

Msgbox right(myString,7)
'will return the 7 characters from the
right side of myString
'Cricket
Msgbox left(myString,6)
'will return the 6 characters from the
left side of myString
'Sachin
```

```
Msgbox mid(myString,8,5)
'will return the 5 characters from the
8th position of myString
'Plays
```

Syntax -

Second parameter in left and right function tells how many characters to return from the string.

In mid functions there are 2 parameters. First parameter tells from which position of the string we have to get the characters and second parameter tells how many characters to return.

5.2 Converting Case of Strings

We can convert the string from lower case to upper case and vice versa using ucase and lcase functions in VBScript.

```
str = "We are learning strings in
VBScript"
Msgbox lcase(str)
'It will print - we are learning strings
in vbscript

Msgbox ucase(str)
'It will print - WE ARE LEARNING STRINGS IN
VBSCRIPT
```

5.3 Replacing part of the string

Replace function can be used to replace the part of the string with other string. Syntax of replace is given below.

Replace(mainString,stringToFind,replaceString[,start_Index
[,Replace_count[,comparison_mode]]])

More information on the parameters is given below.

1. mainString - This is the original string
2. stringToFind - This is the string which will be searched and replaced
3. replaceString - This is the string which will replace other string in the original string
4. start_Index - Index position of the original string from where you have to search it
5. Replace_Count - How many occurrences of the string you want to replace
6. Comparison_Mode - Binary (Case Sensitive) or textual comparison (Case Insensitive). by default it is binary comparison.

Examples -

```
mainString = "Sachin plays cricket"
msgbox
replace(mainString,"Sachin","Arjun")
'Prints Arjun plays cricket.
```

5.4 Finding the length of the string
Len function is used to find the length of the string.

Example -

```
mainString = "Sachin plays cricket"
msgbox len(mainString)
'Prints 20
```

5.5 Trim functions of the string

Trim functions are used to remove the blank spaces from the beginning and ending of the string.

There are 3 functions in this category.

1. ltrim - removes blank spaces from left side of the string
2. rtrim - removes blank spaces from right side of the string
3. trim - removes blank spaces from both left and right side of the string

Example -

```
mainString = "  Sachin plays cricket  "
msgbox ltrim(mainString)
'Prints  "Sachin plays cricket  "

msgbox rtrim(mainString)

'Prints  "  Sachin plays cricket"

msgbox trim(mainString)
'Prints  "Sachin plays cricket"
```

5.6 Reverse the string in VBScript

We can use strreverse function to reverse the string in VBScript.

Example -

```
mainString = "Sachin"
msgbox strreverse(mainString)
'Prints  "nihcaS"
```

5.7 String function in VBScript

We can use string function to get the specified character n times.

Example -

```
msgbox String(5,"*")
'prints *****
```

5.8 Instr function in VBScript

We can use instr function to find the substring in given string. Searching happens from the beginning of the string.

Syntax of Instr

```
InStr([start,]string1,string2[,compare])
msgbox instr(1,"sagaar","g")
'prints 3
```

5.9 Instrrev function in VBScript

We can use instrrev function to find the substring in given string. Searching happens from the end of the string but the position of the character is counted from the beginning of the string.

Syntax of Instrrev

```
InStrRev(string1,string2[,start[,compare
]])
msgbox instrrev("sagaar","g")
'prints 3
```

5.10 Comparing 2 strings in VBScript

We can use **StrComp** function to compare two strings.

The StrComp function returns the values based upon comparison result.

1. -1 (if string1 < string2)
2. 0 (if string1 = string2)
3. 1 (if string1 > string2)
4. Null (if string1 or string2 is Null)

The syntax of the StrComp function is ->

```
StrComp (string1, string2 [,
comparison_mode])
```

The last parameter determines whether comparison is
binary or textual. By default it is binary comparison (Case
Sensitive).

```
msgbox strcomp("Amol","Sagar") 'prints -
1..since ascii value of A is less than
that of S
msgbox strcomp("sagar","sagar")'prints 0
msgbox strcomp("sagar","Amol") 'prints 1
```

6. Maths functions in vbscript

In this chapter, you will learn about math functions in VBScript to find the absolute value of the number, to find the square root of the numbers, to find the round of the number. You will also learn different trigonometric functions.

Below is the list of all maths functions in vb script

1. Abs
2. Atn
3. Cos
4. Exp
5. Fix
6. Int
7. Log
8. Rnd
9. Sgn
10. Sin
11. Sqr
12. Tan
13. round

Let us have a look at each of these functions with

examples.

```
'To find the absolute value
Msgbox Abs(-11) 'prints 11

'To round the number
Msgbox round(22.346,2)   'prints 22.35

'To find the square root of the number
Msgbox Sqr (4)   'prints 2


Msgbox Exp(2)   'e^2
```

Difference between int and fix is that - If the number is negative, int will return smallest possible integer value while fix will return largest possible integer value

For positive numbers, both int and fix work the same way.

```
Msgbox Int (-8.4)   ' returns -9
Msgbox Fix(-8.4) 'returns  -8

'Calculates natural logarithm to the
base e
Msgbox Log(10)

'gets the random number
Msgbox Rnd()

'We must use Randomize function before
Rnd to get different values
```

```
'To get the random numbers between 2
integers
max=100
min=1
Randomize
Msgbox (Int((max-min+1)*Rnd+min))
```

This functions returns the integer number -1,0 or 1 depending upon the sign of the number.

If the sign of the number is negative, -1
if the number is zero , 0
If the sign of the number is positive, 1

```
Msgbox Sgn(-11)   'prints -1
'Used for geometric calculations
Msgbox Sin(90)
Msgbox Tan(45)
Msgbox Atn(45)
Msgbox Cos(0)
```

7. Date time functions in vb script

In this chapter, you will learn about different date and time functions that can be used to find the current date and time of the system, find the future/ past date, find the difference between 2 dates.

It is very important that you know how to work with date and time in VBScript as most of the VBScript programs will have date and time involved in it.

Below is the list of all date and time functions in vb script.

1. date
2. dateadd
3. datediff
4. datepart
5. dateserial
6. datevalue
7. day
8. hour
9. minute
10. second
11. month
12. monthname
13. time
14. timeserial
15. timevalue
16. weekday

17. weekdayname

18. year

We are going to have a look at each of these functions and examples in VBScript.

```
'To find current system date
msgbox " Current System date is -> " &
date
'*****************************************
********'To find the future or past date
msgbox "Tommorrow's date will be " &
dateadd("d",1,date)
```

First argument is Interval Type and it can be of below types.

yyyy - Year

m - Month

d - Day

h - Hour

n - Minute

s - Second

```
'To find the difference between 2 dates
msgbox "Day Difference between today and
tommorrow is " & datediff("yyyy","9-jan-
1986",date)
```

First argument is Interval Type and it can be of below types.

yyyy - Year

m - Month

d - Day

h - Hour

n - Minute

s - Second

```
'To find the current day like 1,2,3...28
msgbox "Current day is -> " & day(date)

'*****************************************
'To find the current hour
msgbox "current hour is -> " & hour(now)

'*****************************************
'To find the current minute
msgbox "current minute is -> " &
minute(now)

'*****************************************
'To find the current second
msgbox "current second is -> " &
second(now)
'*****************************************

'To find the current month number like
1,2....11,12
msgbox "current month is -> " &
month(now)

'*****************************************

'To find the month name like Jan,
Feb.....Dec
msgbox "current month name is -> " &
monthname(month(now))
```

```vbscript
'*******************************************

'To find the current system time
msgbox "current time is -> " & time
'*******************************************


'To find the weekday number like
1,2....7
msgbox "current weekday is -> " &
weekday(now)
'*******************************************


'To find the name of week day like
sunday, monday...saturday
msgbox "current weekday Name is -> " &
weekdayname(weekday(now))
'*******************************************


'To find the current year
msgbox "current year is ->" & year(now)
'*******************************************


'To find the parts of the given time
stamp .equivalent to day, minute,hour,
second etc
msgbox "Day part of the current
timestamp" & datepart("d",now)

'*******************************************
'To convert the string to date
msgbox "String to date -> " &
datevalue("09-jan-1986")
'*******************************************


'To convert the string to time
msgbox "String to time-> " &
TimeValue("7:15:49 PM")
'*******************************************
```

```
'To create date from numbers
msgbox dateserial(1986,01,09)
'**************************************

'To create time from numbers
msgbox timeserial(17,01,09)
```

8. Procedures in VBScript.

> *In this chapter, you will learn about procedures, their uses, passing arguments to the procedures and calling them.*

8.1 What is Procedure?

Sub procedures are used to perform the specific task. Sub procedures are used to increase the reusability of the code.

Simple example of the procedure

Suppose you want to find the sum of 2 numbers. Without procedures, you will write below code.

```
a = 10
b = 20
c = a+ b
Msgbox  c
```

To add another 2 different numbers, you will use below code

```
a = 33

b = 65
c = a+ b
Msgbox  c
```

In above examples, we have to add 2 numbers. So the operation is same (Repeating) So we can write the procedure which will take 2 parameters as shown below.

```
sub sum(byref a, byref b)

    msgbox cint(a) + cint(b)

end sub
```

8.2 Calling procedures in VBScript

To call the procedures we can use below statements.

```
Call sum(10,20)
Call sum(33,65)
```

Thus we can call procedures many times in the code. This reduces the lines of code as well as maintainability of the code.

8.3 Passing arguments to the procedure

We can pass the arguments to the procedure by 2 ways.

1. Pass by reference
2. Pass by value

Pass by reference

By default, values are passed to the procedure by reference. When we pass the values by reference the changes made to the variables in the called procedure are reflected in the calling procedure.

When we pass the arguments to the procedure by reference, the address of the argument variables are passed so less memory is required.

Below Example will demonstrate how we can use Pass by reference.

```
a = 10
call findsqr(a)
msgbox a   'prints 100

sub findsqr(byref a)

  a = a*a

  msgbox a    'prints 100

end sub
```

Pass by value

When we pass the values by value, the changes made to the variables in the called procedure are not reflected in the calling procedure. More memory is required when we pass the arguments to the procedure by value as the copies of the arguments are created in the memory.

Below Example will demonstrate how we can use Pass by Value.

```
a = 10
call findsqr(a)
msgbox a    'prints 10
sub findsqr(byval a)
  a = a*a
  msgbox a    'prints 100
end sub
```

9. Functions in VBScript

In this chapter, you will learn about functions, their uses, passing arguments to the functions and calling them.You will also learn about different built-in functions in VBScript. In the end, we will see the difference between procedures and functions.

9.1 What is Function?

Functions are used to perform the specific task.Functions are used to increase the reusability of the code. Functions are similar to the procedures except one difference that functions can return value. Every function takes input in the form of arguments and produces the output which can be returned to the calling function.

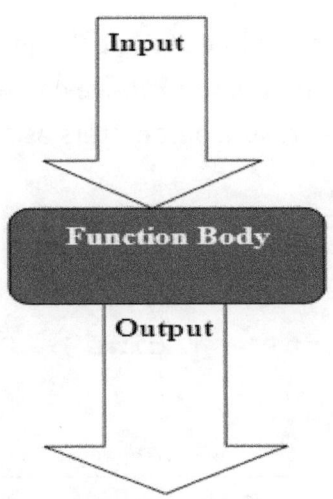

Figure 3 - Functions in VBScript

Simple example of the function

Suppose you want to find the sum of 2 numbers. Without functions, you will write below code.

```
a = 10
b = 20
c = a+ b
Msgbox c
```

To add another 2 different numbers, you will use below code

```
a = 33
b = 65
c = a+ b
Msgbox c
```

In above examples, we have to add 2 numbers. So the operation is same (Repeating) So we can write the function which will take 2 parameters as shown below.

```
function sum(byref a, byref b)

    sum = cint(a) + cint(b)

end function
```

9.2 Calling functions in VBScript

To call the functions we can use below statements.

```
c = sum(10,20)
msgbox c
c =   sum(33,65)
msgbox c
```

Thus we can call functions many times in the code. This reduces the lines of code as well as maintainability of the code.

9.3 Passing arguments to the function

We can pass the arguments to the function by 2 ways.

1. Pass by reference
2. Pass by value

Pass by reference

By default, values are passed to the function by reference. When we pass the values by reference the changes made to the variables in the called function are reflected in the calling function/procedure.

```
a = 10
c = findsqr(a)
msgbox a   'prints 100
msgbox c   'prints 100

function findsqr(byref a)

  a = a*a
```

```
    findsqr = a

end function
```

Pass by value

When we pass the values by value, the changes made to the variables in the called function are not reflected in the calling procedure or function.

```
a = 10
c = findsqr(a)
msgbox a    'prints 10
msgbox c    'prints 100

function findsqr(byval a)

  a = a*a

  findsqr = a

end function
```

9.4 Important built-in functions in VBScript

1. msgbox
2. inputbox
3. eval
4. execute

msgbox function is used to show message to the user.

inputbox function is used to read the value from the user.

```
a = inputbox("Enter the number")
msgbox a 'prints 33
```

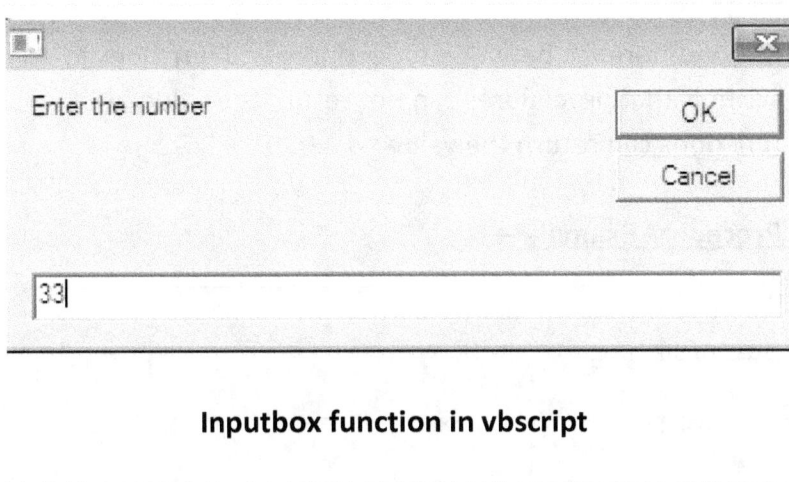

Inputbox function in vbscript

Eval and execute functions are used to execute any valid vbscript expression. Difference between 2 functions is that the operator = is handled in different ways.

Eval always uses = as a comparison operator.
Execute always uses = as a assignment operator.

```
a=20
msgbox eval("a=10")   'will print false
msgbox a

a=20
execute("a=10")
```

```
msgbox a        'will print 10
```

9.5 Difference between Functions and Procedures

Major difference between procedures and functions in vb script is that procedures can not return the value but functions can return the value.

Procedure Example –

```
Sub findsq()

    temp = InputBox("Please enter the
number", 1)
    MsgBox "square root of the num is " &
sqrt(temp)

End Sub
```

Function Example

```
a = findsq()   ' function returns the
value in variable a
msgbox a

function findsq()
  temp = InputBox("Please enter the
number", 1)
  findsq = sqrt(temp)
```

```
End function
```

10. Classes in VBScript

In this chapter, you will learn about how to define the classes in VBScript, create objects of the classes and how to define the constructors and destructors.

10.1 What is class?

Here is an example that shows how we can create a class in VBScript. Once we define the class, we can create its objects and then access its method and properties.

Using a class we can design the VBScript applications with object oriented paradigm.

10.2 Class Example in VBScript

```
'declare the class book.
Class Book

dim bn,bp
'class has 2 variable members bn and bp.

public Property Get bookname()
    ' Get bookname property gets the
book name of the object of Book
  bookname = bn
End Property

public Property Let  bookname(x)
  bn = x
   ' Let  bookname property assigns
value to the book name of the object of
Book
End Property

public Property Get price()
```

```vbscript
price = bp
End Property

public Property Let   price(x)
bp = x
End Property


function  discountedPrice()
Msgbox bp-20
'We can have functions and procedures
inside class to process memeber
variables
End function


Private Sub Class_Initialize    ' Setup
Initialize event.

MsgBox("Object of Book Class created")

End Sub

Private Sub Class_Terminate     ' Setup
Terminate event.

MsgBox("Object of Book Class destroyed")

End Sub

End Class

'*****************************************
Set b1 = new Book
'createing the object b2 of the class
Book.

b1.bookname = "VBSCRIPT Tutorials"
```

```
b1.price = 220
'assigning value to the object b1

Msgbox b1.bookname()
'getting the value of the property
bookname.

'accessing the function in class
b1.discountedPrice()

Set b1 = nothing
```

10.3 Constructors and Destructors in VBScript

VBScript does support object oriented programming to some extent. We can create constructors and destructors in vbscript classes using class_initialize and class_terminate methods. class_initialize method acts like constructor function which gets called automatically when we create an object of the class. This is how we can create and use the classes in VBSCRIPT.

11. Regular Expressions in Vbscript

In this chapter, you will learn about how to use regular expressions in VBScript to find out the matching patterns in the given string. You will also know how to replace the matched pattern.

11.1 Definition
A regular expression is a pattern of characters(meta characters and special characters).

11.2 Applications of Regular Expressions

Regular expressions are used for -
1. Pattern Matching in Strings
2. To find the occurrences of one string/pattern in given string.
3. To replace the patterns with another string in a given text

All programming languages support the use of regular expressions.

11.3 Examples on Regular Expressions
As I said earlier We use regular expressions to check if the given string matches the specified pattern.
For example - Consider a scenario where you have to validate that the given string should be a valid email address.

So list of valid email addresses are -
reply2sagar@gmail.com, ayx@jjjj.in etc

Some of the invalid email addresses are -
kjkjj@fdff, @dfdf.in etc

With the help of regular expression, you can easily validate
the email address.

Syntax of Regular Expression in VBScript:
To write any VBScript program involving regular
expressions, you will have to follow below steps.
1. Create a regular expression object (RegExp)
2. Define the pattern using RegExp object's pattern
property.
3. Use test method to check whether the given string
matches with the pattern specified in step 2.

```
'Create the regular expression object
Set myRegEx = New RegExp

'Specify the pattern (Regular
Expression)
myRegEx.Pattern = "[a-z0-9]+@[a-z]+\.[a-
z]+"

'Specify whether the matching is to be
done with case sensitivity on or off.
myRegEx.IgnoreCase = True

'Use Test method to see if the given
string is matching with the pattern
isMatched =
myRegEx.Test("reply2sagar@gmail.com")

Variable isMatched will be true if the
string "reply2sagar@gmail.com" matches
with the given pattern
"[a-z0-9]+@[a-z]+\.[a-z]+"
```

Another example on Regular Expression.
searchString = "Sachin tendulkar is the master blaster.
Sachin lives in Mumbai and likes to play cricket."

```
searchString = "Sachin"
  Set reObject= New RegExp          '
Create a regular expression.

  reObject.Pattern = searchPattern   '
Set pattern.
  reObject.IgnoreCase = True         '
Set case insensitivity.
  reObject.Global = True
' Set global applicability.
  Set Matches =
reObject.Execute(searchString)      '
Execute search.

  For Each M in Matches

    Str= Str &  M.Firstindex &"->" &
M.Value &   vbCRLF

  Next

  Msgbox   Str

  Msgbox "String after replacing -> " &
vbcrlf  &
reObject.replace(searchString,"Arjun")
```

11.4 Meta characters in regular expressions

1. \ - indicates that the next character would be a special character, a literal or a backreference
2. ^ - Input String should be matched at the beginning.
3. $ - Input String should be matched at the end.
4. * - Matches the preceding character zero or more times. It is same as {0,}.
5. + - Matches the preceding character one or more times. It is same as {1,}.
6. ? - Matches the preceding character zero or one time. It is same as {0,1}
7. {i} - Matches the previous character exactly i times.
8. {i,} - Matches the previous character at least i times and at most any time.
9. {i,j} -Matches the previous character at least i times and at the most j times.
10. . - Matches any single character except "\n".
11. (pattern) - Matches pattern and captures the match that can be used in backreferences.
12. p|q - Matches either p or q. Please note that p and q could be more complex regular expressions.
13. [pqr] - A character set. Matches any one of the character inside the brackets.
14. [^pqr] - A negative character set. Matches any character not inside the brackets.
15. [p-z] - A range of characters. Matches any character in the specified range i.e p,q,r,....x,y,z.
16. [^p-z] - A negative range characters. Matches any character not in the specified range i.e.

a,b,c...m,n,o

1. \b - Matches the boundary of the word

2. \B - Matches middle part of the word.

3. \d   - Matches a digit character. same as [0-9].

4. \D   - Matches a nondigit character. same as [^0-9].

5. \f , \n and \r   - Matches a form-feed character, newline and carriage character.

6. \s   - Matches any white space character including space, tab, form-feed. Equivalent to [\f\n\r\t\v].

7. \S   - Matches any non-white space character. Equivalent to [^ \f\n\r\t\v].

8. \t , \v - Matches a horizontal and vertical tab character.

9. \w   - Matches alpha numeric character including underscore. Equivalent to '[A-Za-z0-9_]'.

10. \W   - Matches any non - alpha numeric character. Equivalent to '[^A-Za-z0-9_]'.

11. \number- A reference back to captured matches.

Some examples on regular expressions:

1. To match the 10 digit mobile number -> \d{10}
2. To match email address -> \w+@\w+\.\w+

Please give your inputs, suggestions, feedback to Us about above VBScript topic. We value your thoughts.

12. Dictionary in VBScript

> *In this chapter, you will learn about the dictionary object and its various methods and properties that help us to add and remove the data in the dictionary. We will also see the difference between array and dictionary in VBScript.*

Dictionary object is used to store the data in key-item pairs in VBScript. A Dictionary object is just like an associative array.
It stores the data in the form of key-item pairs.
Each key has some data item associated with it.
Key can be integer or string format.
Data item can be integer or string or array of variants. It may contain other dictionary itself.

12.1 Methods of Dictionary Object

1. *Add ---------> Adds new key-item pair in the dictionary object*
2. *Exists --------> returns true if the given key exists in the dictionary object*
3. *Items --------> returns the array containing all items in the dictionary object*
4. *Keys --------> returns the array containing all keys in the dictionary object*
5. *Remove -----> removes the key-item pair with given key from the dictionary object*
6. *RemoveAll --> removes all key-item pairs from the dictionary object*

12.2 Properties of Dictionary Object

1. Count-----------> returns the total number of keys in the dictionary object.
2. Item-------------> assigns or returns the item value with given key from the dictionary object.
3. Key-------------> sets the new key value for the given key
4. CompareMode -> assigns or returns the comparison mode for comparing string keys in a Dictionary object.

12.3 Example with dictionary object

Below example will illustrate how to use dictionary in VBScript.

```
'create new dictionary object
Set dictionaryObject =
CreateObject("Scripting.Dictionary")

    dictionaryObject.CompareMode = 1

    'add some key-item pairs
    dictionaryObject.Add "1", "Sagar"
    dictionaryObject.Add "2", "Amol"
    dictionaryObject.Add "3", "Ganesh"

    dictionaryObject.Key("3")  = "Bro"
```

```
    Msgbox dictionaryObject.Item("Bro")

    Msgbox dictionaryObject.Item("bro")

If  dictionaryObject.Exists("1") Then
    Msgbox "Dictionary contains key 1"
Else
    Msgbox "Dictionary does not contain
key 1"
End If

'Display keys and items  in the
dictionary
for each k in dictionaryObject.keys

    Msgbox k &"-"&dictionaryObject.item(k)

next

'Display items
for each i in dictionaryObject.items

    Msgbox  i

next

Msgbox "Total number of keys in the
dictionary are -> " &
dictionaryObject.Count


'Remove the key-item pair with key = 1
from the dictionary object
dictionaryObject.Remove("1")

'Remove all key-item pairs from the
dictionary object
```

```
dictionaryObject.RemoveAll

'Release the object
Set dictionaryObject = nothing
```

12.4 Difference between dictionary and array

Both array and dictionary are used to store the data. But we have below differences in them.

1. Everytime we use array, we have to give the dimensions of the array. But in dictionary we do not need to give the dimensions.
2. We can remove the key-item pair from the dictionary at any point of time to release the memory but in static arrays we can not do it.
3. Data in the array is stored in sequential manner while in the dictionary it is stored in key-item pair.

13. File System in VBScript

In this chapter, you will learn how to use file system object to create, edit, delete files and folders in VBScript. You will also know how to get the information of the drives in the system.

Filesystemobject can be used to work with drives, folders, and files.Filesystemobject has methods and properties that allow us to create, delete, gain information about, and generally manipulate drives, folders, and files.

Important Methods of filesystemobject in vb script

1. CopyFile
2. CopyFolder
3. CreateFolder
4. CreateTextFile
5. DeleteFile
6. DeleteFolder
7. DriveExists
8. FileExists
9. FolderExists
10. GetAbsolutePathName
11. GetBaseName
12. GetDrive
13. GetDriveName
14. GetExtensionName
15. GetFile
16. GetFileName

17. GetFolder
18. GetParentFolderName
19. GetSpecialFolder
20. GetTempName
21. MoveFile
22. MoveFolder
23. OpenTextFile

13.1 Working with files

Creating and writing to file
You can create a text file using this object.

```
Set obj=
createobject("scripting.filesystemobject
")
set f =
obj.createtextfile("g:\salunke.txt")
' create a file
f.write str   ' write some data into file
set f= nothing   ' release memory
set obj = nothing
```

Reading from the file character by character

```
Set fo= createobject("scripting.filesyst
emobject")
set stream1=
fo.OpenTextFile("c:\abc.txt",1)
```

```
msgbox stream1.AtEndOfStream

  Do While    (stream1.AtEndOfStream <>
true )
      msgbox stream1.Read(1)
  loop
      stream1.Close
  Set stream1 = nothing
```

Appending data to file

```
set stream1=
fo.OpenTextFile("c:\abc.txt",8)
   stream1.Write("append it")

  stream1.Close
  Set stream1 = nothing
  Set fo = nothing
```

Delete a text file

```
Set fso =
CreateObject("Scripting.FileSystemObject
")
  fso.DeleteFile("c:\myfile.txt")
Set fso = Nothing
```

13.2 Working with Folders

We can create, delete and copy folders using file system object.

Example to check if the folder exists or not.

```
Set Fo =
createobject("Scripting.FilesystemObject
")
If Not Fo.FolderExists("c:\xyz")) Then
  msgbox "Folder does not exist"
Else
  msgbox  "Folder does exist"
End If
```

Example to create the folder.

```
Set Fo =
createobject("Scripting.FilesystemObject
")
If Not Fo.FolderExists("c:\abc")) Then
   Fo.CreateFolder  ("c:\abc")
End If
```

Example to delete the folder.

```
Set fso =
CreateObject("Scripting.FileSystemObject
")
  fso.DeleteFolder("c:\myfolder")
Set fso = Nothing
```

Example to copy the folder.

```
Set Fo =
createobject("Scripting.FilesystemObject
")

Fo .CopyFolder
"c:\mydocuments\letters\abc",
"c:\tempfolder"

Set Fo = Nothing
```

13.3 Working with Drives

Below example will illustrate how to find the information of the drives in VBScript.

```
Dim fso, d, s

drvPath="d:"

Set fso =
CreateObject("Scripting.FileSystemObject
")
    Set d =
fso.GetDrive(fso.GetDriveName(drvPath))

    msgbox " Volume name of D drive -->"
&   d.VolumeName    & vbcrlf

    msgbox  " Free Space on D drive -->"
& FormatNumber(d.FreeSpace/1024, 0)
```

14. Error Handling

> *In this chapter, you will learn how to use Err object to find the errors in the code and how to ignore errors in the VBScript in production environment.*

VBScript provides below statements and keywords to handle errors.

1. Err object - err.description, err.number
2. on error resume next
3. on error goto 0

14.1 Err Object

Sample code to handle the error is given below

```
If err.number <> 0 Then

    Msgbox err.description
else
    Msgbox "there  was  no  error  in  above
statement"

end if
```

Whenever any error occurs in the script, We get the message window with detailed description of the error.

But when we are executing the scripts, we do not want this message box to appear to come as this will halt the execution of the script.

14.2 On error resume next

To prevent message box from appearing, we use below statement above the block of code.

On error resume next

----

more statements

With On error resume next in place, VBScript runs even though error exists in the code. We can capture those errors using Err object as stated earlier.

When you are debugging the scripts, you should not use On error resume next statement as it will suppress the errors and you will not be able to figure out the issue in your script.

14.3 On error goto 0

On error resume next will suppress all errors in the code. To enable error messages again in the code, you can use the statement.

On error goto 0

This statement will trigger the error message if any error occurs in the code.

15. WSH

In this chapter, you will learn about WSH (Windows Scripting Host).

15.1 Introduction to WSH

Windows Script Host (WSH) is a Windows administration tool.WSH creates an environment for hosting scripts. WSH decides which scripting engine should be used to execute particular script. For example – We can have scripts in many languages like VBScript, Jscript, Perl etc. When we try to execute any of these scripts, WSH will launch proper scripting engine which will execute the script.

WSH is language-independent for WSH-compliant scripting engines.

WSH Objects and Services

Windows Script Host provides several objects for direct manipulation of script execution, as well as helper functions for other actions. Using these objects and services, you can accomplish tasks such as the following:

1. Print messages to the screen

2. Run basic functions such as CreateObject and GetObject

3. Map network drives

4. Connect to printers

5. Retrieve and modify environment variables

15.2 First WSH script

Now let us try to create a simple WSH script. The beauty of the WSH script is that we can create the script in any language like VBScript, Perl, Jscript, and Python and club them together in the wsf file.

We can use notepad to write the WSH Scripts. We can write any wsf script in any language.

Important points to note about wsf file are –

1. WSF file may contain one or more jobs marked by job tag.
2. If there are multiple jobs, root tag should be package.
3. Each job may contain scripts from different language like VBScript and Jscript.
4. WSF is language independent.

General structure of the wsf script is –

```
<Package>

        <job id="1">
                ...scripts
        </job>

        <job id="2">
                ...scripts
```

```
      </job>

</Package>
```

You can execute the wsf file by 2 ways.
1.   Double click on the wsf file.
2.   Run it from command line using cscript command

When you execute the wsf file containing multiple jobs, by default first job in the file is executed. If there is not even a single job in the wsf file, you will get error saying – no jobs are defined in the file.

```
<package>
<job id="first">
<script language="JScript">
 function abc()
{
   wscript.echo ("This is JScript
code called by VBScript");
}
</script>
<script language="VBScript">
      WScript.Echo "This is VBScript
code"
      Call abc()
</script>
</job>
<job id="second">
<script language="VBScript">
```

```
     WScript.Echo "This is second
job"
</script>

</job>
</package>
```

In above wsf file , we have 2 jobs with ids first and second. First job is written in Jscript language while second one is written in VBScript.

If you want to execute specific job in the file, you can use below syntax to run it from command line.

Below command line will execute the job with id – second from the file abc.wsf

```
cscript //Job:second abc.wsf
```

To execute multiple jobs, you can use below command line

```
Cscript //Job:first //Job:second
abc.wsf
```

You can use below javascript code to read or write to standard input and output streams.

```
var x = WScript.StdIn.ReadLine();
WScript.echo (x);
WScript.stdout.WriteLine("you
entered" + x);
```

WSF files have below features.

1. Include script files in the wsf file.
2. Club different script files together.
3. We can add constants to our code.
4. We can edit files with XML editor.
5. Store multiple jobs in single file.

We can include the files in WSF file as shown in below example. We have included file viz. ext.vbs So we can call the functions defined in the ext.vbs. We have called the function – external from WSF file.

```
<job id="IncludeExample">

    <script language="VBScript"
src="ext.vbs"/>
    <script language="VBScript">
      call external()
    </script>

</job>
```

Contents of ext.vbs are –

```
function external()
      msgbox "external function"
end function
```

15.3 WSH Object Model

The following table is a list of the WSH objects and the typical tasks associated with them.

Object	What you can do with this object
Wscript	• Set and retrieve command line arguments • Determine the name of the script file • Determine the host file name (wscript.exe or cscript.exe) • Determine the host version information • Create, connect to, and disconnect from COM objects • Sink events • Stop a script's execution programmatically • Output information to the default output device (for example, a dialog box or the command line)
WshArguments	Access the entire set of command-line arguments
WshNamed	Access the set of named command-line arguments

WshUnnamed	Access the set of unnamed command-line arguments
WshNetwork	• Connect to and disconnect from network shares and network printers • Map and unmap network shares • Access information about the currently logged-on user
WshController	Create a remote script process using the Controller method **CreateScript**()
WshRemote	• Remotely administer computer systems on a computer network • Programmatically manipulate other programs/scripts
WshRemote Error	Access the error information available when a remote script (a WshRemote object) terminates as a result of a script error
WshShell	• Run a program locally • Manipulate the contents of the registry • Create a shortcut • Access a system folder

	• Manipulate environment variables (such as WINDIR, PATH, or PROMPT)
WshShortcut	Programmatically create a shortcut
WshSpecialfolders	Access any of the Windows Special Folders
WshURLShortcut	Programmatically create a shortcut to an Internet resource
WshEnvironment	Access any of the environment variables (such as WINDIR, PATH, or PROMPT)
WshScriptExec	Determine status and error information about a script run with Exec() Access the StdIn, StdOut, and StdErr channels

15.4 WScript Object in WSH

Wscript object can be used to perform below operations.

1. Access command line arguments using **Arguments** property.
2. To get the Version and BuildVersion of WSH.

3. To get the path of the host executable (Wscript.exe/cscript.exe) using Name, FullName, Path properties.
4. To set the script mode using Interactive property (Batch/Interactive).
5. To get the script name using ScriptFullName and ScriptName properties.
6. Access standard streams for input, output and error using StdIn, StdOut, StdErr properties.
7. To connect to specific object using ConnectObject.
8. To disconnect from specific object using DisconnectObject.
9. To create a new object using CreateObject.
10. To display the message to user using Echo method.
11. To get the object using GetObject method.
12. To end the program using Quit method
13. To suspend the execution of the program using Sleep method.

15.5 WshShell Object in WSH

Shell object can be used to do below things in WSH.

1. Creating Shortcuts using CreateShortcut Method
2. Access Special Folders using SpecialFolders Property
3. Reading, writing and deleting registry using RegRead, RegWrite and RegDelete Methods
4. Get Current working directory using CurrentDirectory Property

5. Get Environment variables using Environment Property
6. Send Keys using SendKeys Method
7. Show pop up using Popup Method
8. Launch program in spate process using Run method
9. Launch program in child command shell using Exec method
10. Activate any application window using AppActivate Method
11. Get the actual value of environement variables using ExpandEnvironmentStrings Method
12. Log the events using LogEvent Method

<u>Launching an Application using shell object.</u>

We can launch any application using Run Method of shell object. In below example, we have opened Notepad

```
Set WshShell =
WScript.CreateObject("WScript.Shell
")
WshShell.Run "%windir%\notepad " &
WScript.ScriptFullName
```

The following VBScript code does the same thing, except it specifies the window type, waits for Notepad to be shut down by the user, and saves the error code returned from Notepad when it is shut down.

```
Set WshShell =
WScript.CreateObject("WScript.Shell
")
Return = WshShell.Run("notepad " &
WScript.ScriptFullName, 1, true)
```

Example on Exec Method to launch calculator

```
Dim WshShell, oExec

Set WshShell =
CreateObject("WScript.Shell")

Set oExec = WshShell.Exec("calc")

Do While oExec.Status = 0
     WScript.Sleep 100
Loop

WScript.Echo oExec.Status
```

Example on Popup Method

Popup method is used to show the dialog box to user.

Syntax of this method is given below.

Popup(title, timeout, text, button types/icon types)

Button Types

Value	Description
0	Show **OK** button.
1	Show **OK** and **Cancel** buttons.
2	Show **Abort**, **Retry**, and **Ignore** buttons.
3	Show **Yes**, **No**, and **Cancel** buttons.
4	Show **Yes** and **No** buttons.
5	Show **Retry** and **Cancel** buttons.

Icon Types

Value	Description
16	Show "Stop Mark" icon.
32	Show "Question Mark" icon.
48	Show "Exclamation Mark" icon.
64	Show "Information Mark" icon.

```
Dim WshShell, BtnCode
Set WshShell = CreateObject("WScript.Shell")
BtnCode = WshShell.Popup("did u watch
TV?", 5, "Choose:", 4 + 32)
Select Case BtnCode
    case 6     msgbox "You have not watched TV"
    case 7     msgbox "when will You watch TV?"
    case -1    msgbox "No reply"
End Select
```

Example on ExpandEnvironmentStrings

```
set WshShell =
WScript.CreateObject("WScript.Shell
")
WScript.Echo "WinDir is " &
WshShell.ExpandEnvironmentStrings("
%WinDir%")
WScript.Echo "Temp Directory is " &
WshShell.ExpandEnvironmentStrings("
%temp%")
```

Example on LogEvent

```
Set WshShell =
WScript.CreateObject("WScript.Shell
")
rc = runLoginScript()      'Returns
true if logon succeeds.
if rc then
```

```
    WshShell.LogEvent 0, "Logon
Script Completed Successfully"
else
    WshShell.LogEvent 1, "Logon
Script failed"
end if
```

15.6 WshArguments object in WSH

Provides access to the entire collection of command-line parameters — in the order in which they were originally entered.

The WshArguments object is a collection returned by the WScript object's Arguments property (WScript.Arguments). Two of the WshArguments object's properties are filtered collections of arguments — one contains the named arguments (querying this property returns a WshNamed object), the other contains the unnamed arguments (querying this property returns a WshUnnamed object). There are three ways to access sets of command-line arguments.

1. You can access the entire set of arguments (those with and without names) with the WshArguments object.
2. You can access the arguments that have names with the WshNamed object.
3. You can access the arguments that have no names with the WshUnnamed object

WshArguments object can be used to perform below operations.

1. Find the total number of command line arguments using Length property (Jscript) or Count method (VBScript).
2. Retrieve specific argument using Item property.
3. To get the collection of named and unnamed arguments using Named and Unnamed properties.
4. To display usage of the script using ShowUsage method.

```
<job>
    <runtime>
        <description>This script
reboots a server</description>
        <named
            name = "Server"
            helpstring = "Server to
run the script on"
            type = "string"
            required = "true"
        />
        <example>Example:
reboot.wsf
/server:scripting</example>
    </runtime>
<script language="VBScript">
If WScript.Arguments.Count <> 1
Then
    WScript.Arguments.ShowUsage
    WScript.Quit
End If
</script>
```

```
</job>
```

15.7 WshNetwork Object in WSH

WshNetwork provides access to the shared resources on the network to which your computer is connected.

You create a WshNetwork object when you want to

1. Connect to network printers using AddWindowsPrinterConnection and AddPrinterConnection Method
2. Disconnect from network printers using RemovePrinterConnection
3. Set the default printer using SetDefaultPrinter Method
4. Iterate through all printers using EnumPrinterConnections
5. Map network shares using MapNetworkDrive
6. Disconnect from network shares using RemoveNetworkDrive Method
7. Iterate through network drives using EnumNetworkDrives
8. Access information about a user on the network

Example to display User and Domain information

```
    Set WshNetwork = CreateObject("WScript.Network")
    msgbox "Domain = " & WshNetwork.UserDomain
    msgbox "Computer Name =
" & WshNetwork.ComputerName
    msgbox "User Name = " & WshNetwork.UserName
```

Example to Map a network drive using network object

```
Dim WshNetwork
Set WshNetwork =
WScript.CreateObject("WScript.Netwo
rk")
WshNetwork.MapNetworkDrive "E:",
"\\Server\Public"
```

Example to display shared drives and shared printer connections.

```
    Set WshNetwork = CreateObject("WScript.Network")
    Set oDrives = WshNetwork.EnumNetworkDrives
    Set oPrinters = WshNetwork.EnumPrinterConnections
    msgbox "Network drive mappings:"


    For i = 0 to oDrives.Count - 1 Step 2
       msgbox "Drive " & oDrives.Item(i) & " =
" & oDrives.Item(i+1)
    Next

    msgbox "Network printer mappings:"
```

```
For i = 0 to oPrinters.Count - 1 Step 2
    msgbox  "Port " & oPrinters.Item(i) & " =
" & oPrinters.Item(i+1)
    Next
```

16. WMI

In this chapter, you will learn about WMI and how we can use it.

16.1 WMI Introduction

WMI stands for windows management instrumentation. It is a management technology for Windows operating system.

WMI complies with the standards set by the Distributed Management Task Force (DMTF).

Using WMI, we can do below things.

1. View, edit settings of desktop and server systems.
2. View, edit settings of applications, networks.
3. Manage resources like disk drives, event logs, files, folders, file systems, networking components, operating system settings, performance data, printers, processes, registry settings, security, services, shares, users, and groups (using WMI class) in the enterprise in a consistent way.

So in short, we can manage any resource (hardware as well as software) in windows based systems.

WMI has 3 layers as mentioned below.

1. Managed resources
2. WMI infrastructure

3. Consumers

A managed resource can be any hardware or software component like computer system, disks, peripheral devices, event logs, files, folders, file systems, networking components, operating system subsystems, performance counters, printers, processes, registry settings, security, services, shared folders, SAM users and groups, Active Directory, Windows Installer, Windows Driver Model (WDM) device drivers, and SNMP Management Information Base (MIB) data.

WMI infrastructure consists of below things.

1. Common Information Model Object Manager (CIMOM). Also called as **WMI service**.
2. Common Information Model (CIM) repository, also known as the **WMI repository**.
3. **WMI providers (dlls)**

Providers are residing in the systemroot\System32\Wbem directory. WMI providers act as an intermediary between the CIMOM and a managed resource. Providers request information from and send instructions to WMI-managed resources on behalf of consumer applications and scripts.

Win32 is one such provider.

Below figure shows the structure of WMI.

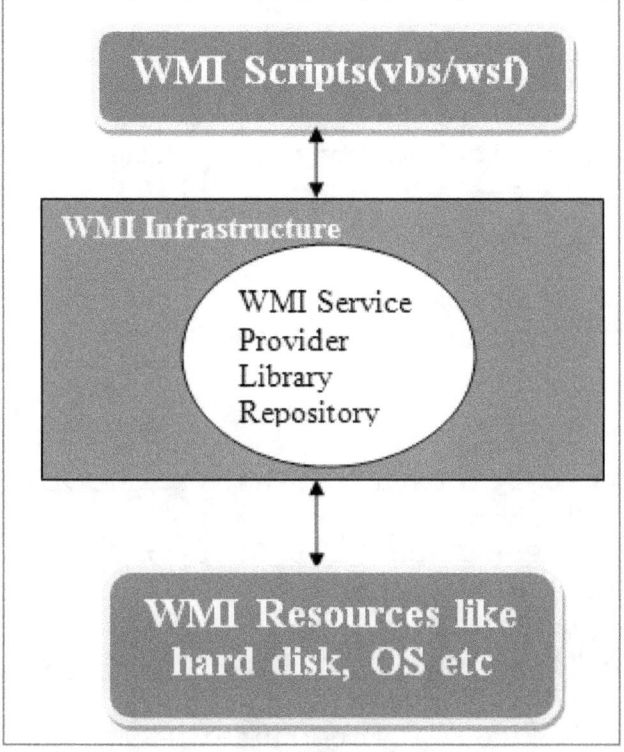

Figure 4 - WMI Infrastructure

16.2 WMI WIN32 Classes

WIN32 providers provides the standard classes created for each system resource. We can find out below information using the script that follows.

1. Which classes are available to me.
2. What are the names of these classes.
3. Which properties and methods can be used with each class.

```
strComputer = "."
Set
objWMIService=GetObject("winmgmts:{imper
sonationLevel=impersonate}!\\" & _
    strComputer & "\root\cimv2")

For Each objclass in
objWMIService.SubclassesOf()
    intCounter=0

'Look for win32 classes
    If Left(objClass.Path_.Class,5) =
"Win32" Then
        For Each Qualifier in
objClass.Qualifiers_
            If
UCase(Trim(Qualifier.Name)) =
"ASSOCIATION" Then
                intCounter = 1
            End If
        Next
        If x = 0 Then
            strComputer = "."
            Set objWMIService =
GetObject _

("winmgmts:{impersonationLevel=impersona
te}!\\" & _
                strComputer &
"\root\cimv2")
            Set strClass =
objWMIService.Get(objClass.Path_.Class)
            Wscript.Echo "PROPERTIES:"
            For each strItem in
strClass.properties_
```

```
                    Wscript.Echo
objClass.Path_.Class & vbTab &
strItem.name
            Next
            Wscript.Echo "METHODS:"
            For Each strItem in
strClass.methods_
                  Wscript.Echo
objClass.Path_.Class & vbTab &
strItem.name
            Next
        End If
    End If
Next
```

16.3 WMI Examples

Now let us have a look at some of the WMI examples.

Close the process by Name using Win32_Process

In below example, we have used WMI to close the internet explorer process.

```
 sComp = "."

'Get the WMI object
Set WMI = GetObject("winmgmts:\\" &
sComp &  "\root\cimv2")

'Get collection of processes for with
name iexplore.exe

Set allIE = WMI.ExecQuery("Select * from
Win32_Process Where Name =
'iexplore.exe'")
```

```
'Loop through each process and terminate
it

For Each IE in allIE

IE.Terminate()

Next
```

Finding the Physical Memory of the system.

```
strComputer = "."

Set objSWbemServices =
GetObject("winmgmts:\\" & strComputer)
Set colSWbemObjectSet = _

objSWbemServices.InstancesOf("Win32_Logi
calMemoryConfiguration")

For Each objSWbemObject In
colSWbemObjectSet
 Wscript.Echo "Total Physical Memory
(kb): " & _
  objSWbemObject.TotalPhysicalMemory
Next
```

Finding the Virtual Memory of the system.

```
strComputer = "."

Set objSWbemServices =
GetObject("winmgmts:\\" & strComputer)
Set colSWbemObjectSet = _
```

```
objSWbemServices.InstancesOf("Win32_Logi
calMemoryConfiguration")

For Each objSWbemObject In
colSWbemObjectSet
 Wscript.Echo "Total Virtual Memory
(kb): " & _
 objSWbemObject.TotalVirtualMemory
Next
```

Getting information about the services in the system using Win32_Service class.

```
strComputer = "."

Set objSWbemServices =
GetObject("winmgmts:\\" & strComputer)
Set colSWbemObjectSet =
objSWbemServices.InstancesOf("Win32_Serv
ice")

For Each objSWbemObject In
colSWbemObjectSet
 Wscript.Echo "Display Name: " &
objSWbemObject.DisplayName & vbCrLf & _
 " State: " & objSWbemObject.State &
vbCrLf & _
 " Start Mode: " &
objSWbemObject.StartMode
Next
```

Showing Windows log information.

```
strComputer = "."
```

```
Set objSWbemServices =
GetObject("winmgmts:\\" & strComputer)
Set colSWbemObjectSet =
objSWbemServices.InstancesOf("Win32_NTLo
gEvent")
For Each objSWbemObject In
colSWbemObjectSet
 Wscript.Echo "Log File: " &
objSWbemObject.LogFile & vbCrLf & _
 "Record Number: " &
objSWbemObject.RecordNumber & vbCrLf & _
 "Type: " & objSWbemObject.Type & vbCrLf
& _
 "Time Generated: " &
objSWbemObject.TimeGenerated & vbCrLf &
_
 "Source: " & objSWbemObject.SourceName
& vbCrLf & _
 "Category: " & objSWbemObject.Category
& vbCrLf & _
 "Category String: " &
objSWbemObject.CategoryString & vbCrLf &
_
 "Event: " & objSWbemObject.EventCode &
vbCrLf & _
 "User: " & objSWbemObject.User & vbCrLf
& _
 "Computer: " &
objSWbemObject.ComputerName & vbCrLf & _
 "Message: " & objSWbemObject.Message &
vbCrLf
Next
```

Showing drive information using Win32_LogicalDisk.

```
strComputer = "."
```

```
Set objSWbemServices =
GetObject("winmgmts:\\" & strComputer)
Set colSWbemObjectSet =
objSWbemServices.InstancesOf("Win32_Logi
calDisk")

For Each objSWbemObject In
colSWbemObjectSet
 Wscript.Echo objSWbemObject.DeviceID
Next
```

Get Free space on the specific hard drive.

```
Set objSWbemServices =
GetObject("winmgmts:")

Set objDisk =
objSWbemServices.Get("Win32_LogicalDisk.
DeviceID='C:'")

Wscript.Echo objDisk.FreeSpace
```